INDIANA

Past and Present

Corona Brezina

rosen publishing's
rosen
central®

New York

Published in 2010 by The Rosen Publishing Group, Inc.
29 East 21st Street, New York, NY 10010

Library of Congress Cataloging-in-Publication Data

Brezina, Corona.
Indiana: past and present / Corona Brezina.—1st ed.
    p. cm.—(The United States: past and present)
Includes bibliographical references and index.
ISBN 978-1-4358-3521-4 (library binding)
ISBN 978-1-4358-8492-2 (pbk)
ISBN 978-1-4358-8493-9 (6 pack)
1. Indiana—Juvenile literature. I. Title.
F526.3.B73 2010
977.2—dc22

2009023685

Manufactured in the United States of America

CPSIA Compliance Information: Batch #LW10YA: For Further Information contact Rosen Publishing, New York, New York at 1-800-237-9932

On the cover: Top left: A female metallurgist determines the temperature of steel in an open-hearth furnace at the Carnegie-Illinois Steel Company in Gary, Indiana, 1943. Top right: An Indiana cornfield is ready for harvest. Bottom: Driver Scott Dixon takes the lead in the Indianapolis 500.

Contents

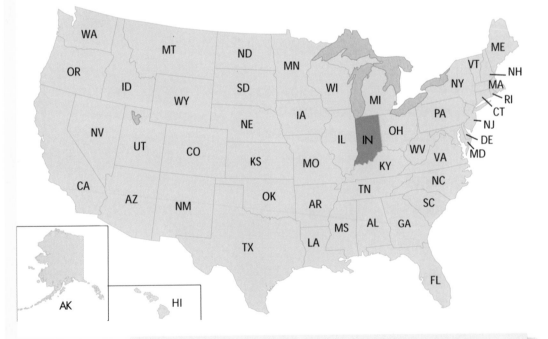

The top map shows Indiana and its immediate neighbors and indicates its largest cities. The bottom map shows Indiana among the nation's other forty-nine states.

Introduction

Indiana is a state with a wealth of natural beauty and resources. It has a long history and has had a significant impact on American culture. Indiana's geographical diversity is impressive. It has rolling sand dunes on its northern Lake Michigan coast, breathtaking caverns to the south, and fertile plains at its center.

The people who have made Indiana their home have been equally impressive, from the earliest days of settlement to the present. Early Native Americans constructed massive mounds that exist to this day. In fact, they are some of the most significant prehistoric sites in the United States. Two presidents, William Henry Harrison and Benjamin Harrison, came from Indiana. So did popcorn magnate Orville Redenbacher and the King of Pop, Michael Jackson.

Indiana's state motto is "The Crossroads of America," due to the state's role as a centrally located transportation hub. Many major railways, highways, and waterways pass through Indiana. In addition, the state's agricultural products are shipped nationwide and beyond, helping feed the country and the world. Its industries have helped build America and keep it running, from limestone for buildings and steel for skyscrapers to automobiles, vehicle parts, and financial services.

Indiana is indeed at the crossroads of America. It has helped build the dietary, nutritional, physical, transportation, and financial foundations upon which the nation's prosperity and well-being depend.

Chapter 1

THE GEOGRAPHY OF INDIANA

About five-sixths of Indiana's land was shaped by glaciers. Beginning hundreds of thousands of years ago, these ice sheets crept down from the north during several prehistoric ice ages. In places, the ice sheet was more than 1,000 feet (305 meters) thick. The glaciers flattened hills and filled in valleys. When the last ice age ended about twelve thousand years ago, the glaciers left behind fertile soil and gravel deposits. The melting ice sheets carved out new lakes and rivers. As the climate warmed, forests sprang up across the land that would become known as Indiana.

Before 1800, nearly 90 percent of Indiana was forested. There were also wetlands and prairie grasslands, mostly in the northwestern part of the state. Today, most of the forests have been cleared, some of the wetlands have been drained, and most of the prairie grasslands are gone.

Terrain

With an area of 36,291 square miles (93,993 square kilometers), Indiana ranks thirty-eighth in size among U.S. states. Indiana is part of the Midwestern region of the country. It is also one of the Great Lakes states because of its coastline along Lake Michigan. Indiana is bordered by Ohio to the east, Kentucky to the south, and Illinois to

A classic Indiana farm contributes to the state's agricultural output north of Kokomo, the county seat of Howard County and the site of an early nineteenth-century trading post.

the west. Lake Michigan and the state of Michigan make up the northern border.

Indiana's terrain and climate change from north to south. Its northwestern border consists of a 45-mile-long (72 km) shoreline along Lake Michigan. There are towering sand dunes along much of this stretch. The tallest of these is Mount Baldy, with a height of 123 feet (37.5 m). Farther inland, patches of forest alternate with marshy wetlands. Northwest Indiana is heavily populated because of its convenient proximity to Chicago, Illinois.

Central Indiana contains a region sometimes called the Till Plains. It has rich soil and mostly flat terrain, ideal for growing crops and

The Indiana Dunes

University of Chicago botanist Henry Chandler Cowles was one of the first people to appreciate the unique ecosystem of the Indiana Dunes. Returning to the dunes time after time, he achieved groundbreaking research on plant ecology. In 1899, he published an article explaining how plant life in an area gradually changes because the plants themselves change the environmental conditions around them.

Most people, however, valued the lakeshore as an industrial, rather than ecological, resource. During the early twentieth century, glass manufacturing companies hauled away Indiana's tallest dune, the 200-foot-high (61 m) Hoosier Slide. U.S. Steel and other industries built plants on the shores of Lake Michigan. In response, Cowles helped organize the Prairie Club to advocate preservation of the dunes. After ten years, in 1926, the Indiana Dunes State Park was established. Still, it was only a small protected portion of the 45-mile-long (72 km) lakeshore.

The battle to save the dunes intensified when politicians and businesses proposed building a new Port of Indiana-Burns Harbor. In 1952, Dorothy Buell, head of the Save the Dunes Council, took her campaign nationwide. Illinois Senator Paul Douglas voiced his impassioned support for the cause and introduced a bill in the U.S. Senate to preserve the dunes as a national monument. When the bill failed, he worked tirelessly for a compromise. Meanwhile, the Save the Dunes Council rallied public support and testified before Congress. In 1966, a compromise bill authorized construction of the port, but it also established the Indiana Dunes National Shoreline. Since then, it has been expanded four times to an area of 15,000 acres (61 sq km) containing 15 miles (24 km) of lakefront.

Today, visitors can camp, hike, swim, ride horses, visit historic sites, and even get married at the Indiana Dunes National Lakeshore. Preservation and restoration of natural habitats remains an ongoing concern, however. Also, pollution, development, and invasive species continue to threaten the dunes.

raising livestock. It is part of the Midwestern agricultural area known as the Corn Belt. Indianapolis is located in central Indiana. The original city plan, drawn in 1821, featured streets radiating out from the center of the city, similar to Washington, D.C.

In the southern part of the state, farmland gives way to rugged hills and valleys crossed by occasional small streams. Limestone lies under much of this region, and underground streams have carved out many spectacular caves. Limestone is also used as a building material. The U.S. Capitol, the Pentagon, and the Empire State Building are just a few of the famous buildings that feature Indiana limestone. There are also rich coal reserves in southern Indiana. The Hoosier National Forest covers an area of more than 200,000 acres (809 sq km) across several sites. It gives the public a chance to explore scenic trails and views, sandstone formations, several historic buildings, and Indiana's only designated wilderness area.

Indiana's many lakes and waterways are a valuable resource. One of the state's most economically important waterways is the Port of Indiana-Burns Harbor, an artificial harbor at the southern tip of Lake Michigan. It was constructed so that steel manufacturers and other industries would be better able to transport their products throughout the country and the world. Northern Indiana is dotted with small lakes. Lake Wawasee is the state's largest natural lake. There are also nine large human-made reservoirs throughout Indiana that were formed by damming nearby waterways. The largest of these is Lake Monroe.

The most famous river in Indiana is the Wabash River, which enters from Ohio, meanders southwest across the Hoosier state, then forms a stretch of the Indiana-Illinois border. Many songs and stories, including Indiana's official state song, tell of the Wabash. Another important river is the Ohio River, which forms Indiana's southern

A barge plies the waters of the Ohio River between Henderson, Kentucky, and Evansville, Indiana.

border. It merges with the Wabash River at Indiana's southwest corner. The Ohio River, which is deeper than the Wabash, was an important waterway for pioneer settlement and steamboat travel.

Climate

Indiana has a temperate climate, with typically cold winters and hot summers. Average temperatures tend to be significantly warmer in the southern region of the state. A long growing season and plentiful rainfall contribute to the success of Indiana's crops. The state is particularly beautiful in the fall when the leaves on the trees change color.

The humid climate can lead to muggy summers and sometimes bring severe weather. There are thunderstorms in the summer that can feature thunder, lightning, torrential rain, and even hail. Indiana is generally considered part of the belt of middle American states known as Tornado Alley. In addition, winter blizzards can cause heavy snowfall, especially in the northwest region near Lake Michigan. Here, more than 100 inches (2.5 m) of snow can fall in a single winter. Heavy rain and melting snow sometimes causes severe flooding. In June 2008, Indiana experienced floods that in some regions were the worst in nearly a century.

Wildlife

Indiana is home to many species of trees and prairie plants. Forests and woodlands are made up of hickory, cedar, dogwood, elm, oak, maple, black walnut, birch, buckeye, and tulip poplar, which is the state tree. The types of trees vary from north to south. For example, white pines and tamaracks are common in the north, while persimmons and bald cypresses are found farther south. There are also prairie grasses and plants, such as wild peppermint, oxeye daisies, milkweed, and black-eyed Susans. Common animals include beavers, bobcats, rabbits, coyotes, foxes, bats, muskrat, raccoons, skunks, and white-tailed deer. Pheasant, grouse, wild turkeys, and many songbirds are native to Indiana, and huge flocks of migrating birds pass through the state.

The Indiana Dunes provide a delicate and diverse habitat for more than a thousand species of plants. They are also home to many

Grassy sand dunes, some quite tall, surround the Indiana coastline of Lake Michigan.

different birds, mammals, amphibians, reptiles, fish, butterflies, and dragonflies. There are insect-eating plants such as the pitcher plant, an endangered orchid, and even prickly pear cacti. The dunes themselves are held in place by the roots of plants such as marram grass. The greatest variety of life forms is found inland from the dunes in swamps, ponds, and forests.

According to the U.S. Fish and Wildlife Service, there are thirty-one endangered or threatened species in Indiana—twenty-seven animals and four plants. These include the gray wolf, two bat species, the piping plover, and the eastern cougar, as well as lesser known species such as various types of mussels and insects.

THE HISTORY OF INDIANA

Indiana's history begins thousands of years before statehood. Archaeological evidence indicates that the first humans reached Indiana as long ago as 15000 BCE. They were the first of a succession of different prehistoric Native American cultures. These early residents hunted large game such as mammoth.

The Earliest Residents

Another group, known as the Archaic Tradition, hunted small game, fished, and gathered plant food from 8000 BCE to 1000 BCE. They developed a range of specialized stone tools for tasks such as preparing food. Members of the Woodland Tradition, which lasted from about 1000 BCE to 900 CE, developed agriculture. People started cultivating maize (corn) and squash. They also began creating pottery, and they buried their dead in large burial mounds.

The most complex prehistoric culture was the Mississippian Tradition, which lasted from about 900 to 1600 CE. Its members established villages, cultivated crops extensively, and crafted tools and ornately decorated pottery. This group is also known as the Mound Builders because of their massive burial mounds. Their largest settlement was near present-day Evansville. About three thousand people lived in a large village surrounding a terraced mound 650 feet long (198 m), 300 feet wide (91 m), and 44 feet (13 m) tall.

The Mississippian people left the region; historians do not know why. The next group of Native Americans did not settle in the state until the late seventeenth and early eighteenth centuries. The two major tribes were the Miami and the Potawatomi, who both migrated from the west. The Potawatomi settled in northern Indiana, and the Miami dominated central and southern Indiana. The Wea, Piankashaw, Kickapoo, Kaskaskia, Delaware, Wyandot, and Shawnee also migrated into Indiana.

European Exploration and Settlement

René-Robert Cavelier, Sieur de La Salle, traveled the Mississippi River from present-day Illinois to the Gulf of Mexico.

The first European to explore Indiana was René-Robert Cavelier, Sieur de La Salle. In 1679, he led an expedition from southeastern Lake Michigan as far as present-day South Bend. He then canoed down the Kankakee River into Illinois. Indiana was part of New France at this time, and French fur traders soon began establishing trading posts. Since they only had a small military force, they worked hard to establish friendly relations with Native Americans.

The first post, Ouiatenon, near present-day Lafayette, was built in 1717, and two others followed.

In 1756, Britain declared war on France. There was no fighting in Indiana during the French and Indian War—the British simply occupied the three French posts. The British were victorious. In the 1763 peace treaty, the French ceded all of their North American territory to the British.

Displeased with the new British authorities, several Native American tribes rebelled in 1763. An Ottawa chief named Pontiac laid siege to Detroit for four months and captured most of the trading posts at the northwestern frontier of British territory. However, Pontiac's Rebellion, as it was called, collapsed when his followers eventually lost heart.

The first battles of the American Revolution were fought in 1775, and the Declaration of Independence was written in 1776. The war did not reach Indiana, however, until 1777. Based in Detroit, British Lieutenant Governor Henry Hamilton urged Native American allies to attack American frontiersmen. He supplied them with weapons and food. A young American major named George Rogers Clark came up with a plan to end the raids. In 1778, he recruited troops and marched to take the village of Kaskaskia in present-day Illinois. He won over many Native American allies. Clark also sent a captain to seize the Indiana town of Vincennes, one of the original French posts.

When Hamilton heard of Clark's invasion, he gathered a force and set off to Vincennes. He easily regained control of the lightly defended town. Clark launched a surprise counterattack in February 1779, marching for sixteen days through four flooded valleys to reach Vincennes. After a brief battle, Hamilton surrendered unconditionally. In 1781, Clark tried to capture Detroit. The attempt was unsuccessful, but Clark remains the best-known Revolutionary War figure of what was then known as the Northwest Territory.

The forces of U.S. general Anthony Wayne defeated Native American warriors at the Battle of Fallen Timbers in 1794. This victory opened up the Ohio Valley to white settlement.

Territorial Days

The American Revolution ended in 1781. In 1787, the Northwest Ordinance established a government for the Northwest Territory, the region northwest of the Ohio River and east of the Mississippi River. Native Americans, who resented increasing settlement on their lands, formed a confederacy of tribes to oppose the Americans. They led raids against settlers, and the Americans launched military expeditions in response. After several years of warfare, General Anthony Wayne defeated the Native Americans in 1794 at the Battle of Fallen Timbers. In the 1795 Treaty of Greenville, Native Americans ceded territory including much of what would become Ohio and part of present-day Indiana.

In 1800, Congress divided the Northwest Territory, and the region west of Ohio was renamed the Indiana Territory. William Henry Harrison became governor of the new territory. The Indiana territory shrank nearly to its present-day borders when Michigan became a separate territory in 1805, followed by Illinois in 1809. Meanwhile, Harrison began negotiating treaties with Native Americans. Many tribes yielded their land claims in return for payment. Still, Native Americans grew resentful of the spread of American settlers.

A Shawnee spiritual leader called the Prophet began preaching about the renewal of Native American culture. His brother, a charismatic warrior named Tecumseh, began uniting Native American tribes in resistance. Tecumseh met with Harrison in 1810 to discuss a peaceful resolution, but they did not come to an agreement. In 1911, Harrison moved military forces close to Prophetstown, Tecumseh's stronghold. Although Tecumseh was away, the Prophet unwisely attacked without him, and Harrison declared victory at the Battle of Tippecanoe.

The area's Native Americans lost that battle, but their spirit remained undefeated. Indeed, they sided with the British forces in Canada during the War of 1812. The Americans won the war, however, and Tecumseh was killed during the fighting. The military victory and resulting treaty ended Native American resistance in the Northwest.

Statehood and Growth

In 1816, the Indiana Territorial Assembly met to draft a constitution, taking a step toward statehood. Later that year, Indiana officially became the nineteenth U.S. state. Slavery was already a highly controversial issue—the Indiana Constitution forbade slavery in the new state.

Johnny Appleseed and His Legacy

Everyone has heard the tale of Johnny Appleseed, the man who roamed the countryside planting apple trees. Most people do not realize that he was a real person named John Chapman. Nor do they realize that many of the extraordinary stories told about him are based on fact. There was actually a method behind Chapman's allegedly willy-nilly planting of apple trees. He did not scatter seeds randomly. Instead, he cleared and fenced in a fertile site and established nurseries of trees in frontier areas. This way, when settlers moved nearby, he would have young trees ready to sell. He supplied trees to an area of more than 100,000 square miles (almost 300,000 sq km).

Born in Massachusetts in 1774, Chapman left around 1792 to begin his unconventional business. He began by planting trees in New York and Pennsylvania. In his later life, he traveled mainly in Ohio and Indiana, occasionally venturing into Kentucky and Illinois.

Chapman was a highly unusual, though beloved, character. He became a legend during his own lifetime. Chapman never settled down in a fixed residence. He went barefoot, and some people claimed that he dressed in old coffee sacks. Chapman loved animals, domestic and wild, and he was a vegetarian. He was friendly with Native Americans. He was devoutly religious, believing in the mystic teachings of Emanuel Swedenborg. Chapman often camped outdoors, though settlers considered him a welcome and entertaining guest. He was generous in lending a hand when needed, and he was willing to barter or accept a promise of payment when people couldn't afford to buy his apple trees.

Chapman died in Fort Wayne in 1845. Today, the site believed to be his grave is an official landmark in Johnny Appleseed Park. Every year, the Johnny Appleseed Festival is held in the park during the fall apple harvest season.

Indianapolis eventually became the state capital in 1825. Settlers flocked to the young state, drawn by the fertile, plentiful land. Most newcomers were families who cleared trees and built wood cabins. They cultivated field crops (primarily corn), raised animals (such as cows, pigs, and chickens), kept a garden, and hunted game for extra meat.

Canals, roads, and railroads were built to transport freight and passengers, and first towns and then cities began to grow. Indiana's economy was based on agriculture. The state was among the country's top corn and hog producers well into the twentieth century. Industry—such as the Studebaker Wagon Works—began to grow in the north.

During the 1850s, most Hoosiers (as Indiana residents are known, though the origins of the word are unclear) were opposed to the prospect of war. When the Civil War broke out in 1861, Indiana strongly supported the Union. Thousands of men rushed to enlist when President Abraham Lincoln called for volunteers for the cause. Governor Oliver Morton sent troops and weapons. There was no fighting in Indiana except for an invasion of less than a week by Confederate General John Hunt Morgan, who seized supplies and caused damage to railways.

Growth and Progress

After the end of the Civil War, Indiana saw profound economic and social shifts. Although agriculture remained strong, Indiana became an important manufacturing state. In the 1880s, a natural gas boom in east-central Indiana attracted to that region glass manufacturers and other industries that used gas as a fuel. The natural gas supplies ran out in the 1890s, but the state's industrial base was

A poster announces the 1885 Indiana State Fair, a celebration of the state's agriculture, industry, and education.

firmly established by then. In the northwest, oil refineries and steel works were opened along the Lake Michigan shore, near Gary. U.S. Steel's Gary Works, established in 1909, was the world's largest steel mill. Automobile manufacturing plants were opened in towns and cities across the state.

Factory workers often endured long, hard hours at the job. Labor organizers, such as Indiana native Eugene Debs, encouraged workers to join labor unions in order to improve their pay and working conditions. Some workers, such as coal miners and railroad workers, went on strike to protest dangerous, sometimes deadly, labor conditions.

Newcomers were drawn to Indiana's booming industrial centers. During the early twentieth century, many immigrants from southern and eastern Europe settled in the northern part of the state. A wave of African Americans arrived from the South, many taking jobs in the steel mills. Some white Hoosiers were intolerant of African Americans, and during the 1920s, a hate group, the Ku Klux Klan, was very active in Indiana. Its influence waned during the 1930s.

The Great Depression of the 1930s was a hard time for Indiana's agricultural and manufacturing industries alike. Hoosiers opposed

The skyline of Indianapolis, Indiana's state capital, rises above White Water State Park. It is the state's largest city and the third largest city in the Midwest behind Chicago and Detroit.

entrance into World War II. Yet the war brought increased demand for manufactured items, such as army trucks, airplane engines, ammunition, and other wartime goods.

In the late 1970s, industry began to decline across the region. Indiana became part of the "Rust Belt," as its steel and auto companies closed or cut production.

Indiana has continued to become more ethnically diverse. In 1967, Richard G. Hatcher was elected mayor of Gary, becoming one of the nation's first African American mayors of a large city. Since the early 1990s, Indiana's Hispanic population has grown rapidly.

THE GOVERNMENT OF INDIANA

As is the case in every American state, Indiana is governed at local, state, and federal levels. Local governments provide many everyday services that people take for granted, such as education, policing, and road repairs. There are local governments in six different classifications: counties, townships, municipalities (including cities and towns), school districts, library districts, and special districts, such as fire protection. In total, there are more than three thousand local governments in Indiana.

Most county governments are run by commissioners and a council, all elected. There are ninety-two counties in Indiana. The largest county by population is Marion County, home of Indianapolis. This is followed by Lake County in the northwest and St. Joseph County, the county seat of South Bend. Cities are governed by a mayor and a city council, and towns are governed by a town council that chooses a council president.

Branches of State Government

There are three branches of Indiana state government: the executive, legislative, and judicial branches. All three branches are housed

The Indiana Statehouse in Indianapolis houses the General Assembly, the governor's office, the state supreme court, and other state offices. It is the fifth building to serve as Statehouse.

in the historic Indiana Statehouse (constructed of Indiana limestone, of course).

The governor is the chief executive of the government. Indiana governors serve four-year terms and are limited to two consecutive terms in office. The governor signs—or vetoes—legislation and appoints many state officials. The lieutenant governor is elected as the governor's running mate. Other elected officials in the executive branch include the attorney general, the secretary of state, the treasurer, and the auditor.

Indiana's state legislature—the branch of government that makes laws—is called the General Assembly. It is divided into the

Hoosiers in Washington

William Henry Harrison (1773–1841) became governor of the Indiana Territory in 1800. In 1811, he led American forces against Native Americans at the Battle of Tippecanoe. He went on to serve in the U.S. House of Representatives, the Ohio Senate, and the U.S. Senate as a member of the Whig party. In 1840, he was elected president, running under the slogan "Tippecanoe and Tyler, too." Inauguration day was cold and rainy. He developed pneumonia and died a month later.

His grandson, Benjamin Harrison (1833–1901), won the presidency in 1888. He received more electoral votes than his opponent Democrat Grover Cleveland, though Cleveland won the popular vote. Harrison's presidency was marked by increased international engagement. The domestic economy slumped, however, and Cleveland won the 1892 election.

One of America's greatest presidents, Abraham Lincoln (1809–1865), was born in Kentucky but grew up from the age of seven in a log cabin in southwestern Indiana. The family moved to Illinois in 1830 when Lincoln was twenty-one. Today, the Macon County site is preserved as the Lincoln Boyhood National Memorial.

Indiana has also produced five vice presidents. Schuyler Colfax served from 1869 to 1873 as vice president for President Ulysses S. Grant; Thomas Hendricks for Grover Cleveland (1885); Charles Fairbanks for Theodore Roosevelt (1905–1909); Thomas Marshall for Woodrow Wilson (1913–1921); and Dan Quayle for George H. W. Bush (1989–1993).

John Roberts Jr. currently serves as chief justice of the U.S. Supreme Court. Roberts grew up in northwest Indiana and worked for the government under Reagan and George H. W. Bush.

Grandfather and grandson William Henry Harrison *(left)* and Benjamin Harrison *(right)* both served as U.S. presidents.

Senate and House of Representatives. Senators serve four-year terms; representatives serve two-year terms.

The highest court in Indiana's judicial system is the five-member supreme court. The next highest courts are the tax court and the fifteen-member court of appeals, which is divided into five regional districts with three judges per district. The governor appoints judges to the supreme court and to the court of appeals. After two years, voters decide whether to retain the judge for a ten-year term.

Indiana's first statehouse *(above)* was located in Corydon, the state capital from 1816 to 1825.

Lower courts include circuit courts and superior courts, which operate on a county level. There are also local city and town courts. Large cities may have specialized courts, such as criminal courts or juvenile courts.

National Representation

Indiana is represented in Congress by two U.S. senators, who serve six-year terms. It also has nine U.S. representatives—one from each of nine districts—who serve two-year terms.

Chapter 4

THE ECONOMY OF INDIANA

Indiana has historically been a leading state in agriculture and manufacturing. These sectors remain important, but like the rest of the United States, Indiana has seen a shift toward the service sector, which includes jobs ranging from tourism to financial services. These services are provided by banks, credit card companies, insurance companies, stock brokerage houses, and investment funds.

Industry

Although manufacturing in Indiana has declined since the 1970s, it still makes up a greater share of Indiana's economy than it does in most states. In fact, it employs about one out of five Hoosiers. The state remains the biggest steel producer in the country. Transportation equipment—including automobile and aircraft parts, truck and bus bodies, semitrailers, motor homes, and vehicle assembly—is a major industry.

Indiana is also a major producer of plastics, chemicals, pharmaceuticals, and medical equipment. Indianapolis is home to Eli Lilly and Company, one of the biggest pharmaceutical companies in the world. Although it manufactures drugs to treat health conditions of

Despite the decline in manufacturing and Indiana's place in the Rust Belt, its plants continue to produce steel for use worldwide, particularly in Gary, along the Lake Michigan shore.

all kinds, the company is an industry leader in treatments for various psychiatric disorders. One of its most famous products is the antidepressant Prozac. The company was founded in 1873 by the Hoosier Eli Lilly (1838–1898), a pharmacist and former Union officer. He wanted to produce high-quality drugs that would be prescribed by doctors. This was an innovative practice for his day. Upon Lilly's death, his son took over the company, and control of the business remained in family hands until 1953. Today, Lilly is the tenth largest pharmaceutical company in the world, employing forty thousand people around the globe and selling its products in 143 countries.

The Indy 500

In 1911, several Indianapolis businessmen in the automotive industry sponsored a 500-mile (805 km) car race over Memorial Day weekend at the new Indianapolis Motor Speedway. The track was surfaced with millions of bricks. Driver Ray Harroun won the race driving a Marmon "Wasp," averaging a speed of 74 miles per hour (119 km/hr). He took home a prize of $14,250.

Thus began the Indianapolis 500, the "Greatest Spectacle in Racing." In 1936, the Borg-Warner Trophy was awarded for the first time. Every winner since then has received the trophy.

The Indy 500 was cancelled during the two world wars, and by 1945, the speedway had grown dilapidated. Owner Eddie Rickenbacker sold it to Tony Hulman, a Terre Haute businessman who had made a fortune marketing Clabber Girl baking powder. Hulman spent millions of dollars renovating the track and established many beloved Indy 500 traditions. The 500 Festival Parade, first held in 1957, draws throngs of spectators to downtown Indianapolis every year. Every race begins with the song "Back Home Again in Indiana," ending with a balloon release.

Racing is a dangerous sport, and there have been many tragedies on the Indianapolis Motor Speedway. In 1933, five men were killed. In 1955, two-time Indy 500 winner Bill Vukovich died in a multicar accident while in the lead. In 1973, two drivers and a crewman were fatally injured during the race.

Three racing legends have won the race four times each: A. J. Foyt, Al Unser, and Rick Mears. The youngest race winner, Troy Ruttman, was twenty-two; the oldest, Al Unser, was forty-seven. Five women have raced in the Indy 500.

Today, with about four hundred thousand spectators, the Indy 500 is the world's biggest single-day sports event. Race winners now take home nearly $3 million. The race is such an important part of Indiana's tradition that an Indy car is featured on the 2002 Indiana state quarter.

Agriculture

About three-quarters of Indiana's land area is farmland. There are sixty-three thousand farms, making up 15.4 million acres (6.2 hectares). Yet agriculture only employs a small percentage of Indiana's workforce. Even so, the state is a major producer of crops and livestock. Corn and soybeans are the most important crops by value. Hoosiers also grow vegetables, wheat, hay, apples, and other fruit crops.

An Indiana farmer feeds his pigs locally grown grain. Grain and livestock are some of Indiana's chief exports and a mainstay of the state economy.

Indiana is a top producer of hogs. Other important livestock products include milk products—ice cream, in particular—and eggs.

Indiana is the second largest popcorn producing state in the country. One Hoosier, Orville Redenbacher (1907–1995), studied agronomy at Purdue University. He then spent years developing the perfect fluffy and light variety of popcorn. He and his business partner, Charles Bowman, started marketing it as RedBow popcorn—a combination of their names. However, they eventually changed the name to Orville Redenbacher's Gourmet Popping Corn. Even after the company was sold and Redenbacher had moved away, he would return every year for the annual Popcorn Festival in Valparaiso.

A freight train hauling Indiana coal travels from the mining region in the south of the state. Indiana produces more than 96 percent of its energy through coal-burning power plants.

Mining and Natural Resources

Coal mined in southern Indiana is the state's most important mineral resource. Indiana quarries produce limestone and gravel. There are also oil deposits in Indiana, though oil production is not a significant part of the economy.

Most of Indiana's energy comes from coal-burning power plants. Yet the state is expanding its production of renewable energy sources, such as biofuels. These are fuels derived from organic matter such as plants. Ethanol, for example, is made from corn, and biodiesel is made from soybeans. Indiana also has the potential to expand wind power produced by wind turbines.

Service Sector

The service sector employs about three-quarters of Indiana's work-force. Most service sector jobs are in cities and other densely populated areas. Employees in the service sector range from workers in food service, retail, and customer service to highly trained profes-sionals in information services, insurance, and finance. Education and health care are two of the largest service sectors in the state. Transportation is also an important contributor to the service sector because of the many railroads, ships, and trucking companies that do business in Indiana.

Chapter 5

PEOPLE FROM INDIANA:
PAST AND PRESENT

Indiana has been home to many proud citizens and notable persons, including presidents and other politicians. Yet it has been particularly fertile ground for artists, writers, actors, entertainers, and social and union activists.

Social and Union Activists

Eugene Debs (1855–1926) Labor organizer and Socialist leader Eugene Debs worked in railroad shops and as a locomotive fireman before becoming involved in union activities. He became president of the American Railway Union in 1893 and was imprisoned for his involvement in the 1895 Pullman Strike. Debs also helped found the U.S. Socialist Party and the Industrial Workers of the World. He ran as the Socialist presidential candidate five times.

Theodore Dreiser (1870–1945) Author Theodore Dreiser is best known for his highly realistic novels. These include *Sister Carrie* and *An American Tragedy*, in which ordinary characters are portrayed as being at the mercy of forces out of their control. Dreiser, who grew up in Terre Haute, worked as a journalist, editor, and publisher. Later in life, he became an active social reformer. Dreiser's brother, Paul, wrote the Indiana state song.

Jimmy Hoffa (1913–?) Jimmy Hoffa, born in Brazil, Indiana, served as president of the Teamsters Union from 1957 to 1972. Federal investigators suspected that he was involved in organized crime. In 1964, he was convicted of unrelated charges—jury tampering and fraud. He went to prison in 1967 and was released in 1971 when President Richard Nixon commuted his sentence.

Jimmy Hoffa, then vice president of the Teamsters Union, testifies before a Congressional committee investigating corruption in the union.

Hoffa disappeared in 1975 and is presumed to have been murdered. His body has never been found.

Artists and Writers

Ernie Pyle (1900-1945) Pulitzer Prize–winning journalist Ernie Pyle was one of the most famous and respected World

The Indiana Music Scene

Indiana has a long and proud musical heritage. It was first influenced by the traditions of its early nineteenth-century German and Irish immigrants. Indiana also became one of the first places jazz flourished once it began traveling beyond New Orleans and, then, Chicago. In fact, Indiana gave rise to two of the leading jazz and pop songwriters of the early twentieth century—Cole Porter ("You Do Something to Me," "Begin the Beguine," "Night and Day," "What Is This Thing Called Love?") and Hoagy Carmichael ("Stardust," "Heart and Soul," "Lazy River," "Skylark"). The work of these two men became American standards, sung by the likes of Frank Sinatra, Ella Fitzgerald, Tony Bennett, and Bing Crosby. Their songs are still recorded and performed by jazz and cabaret artists today.

As times changed, so, too, did musical styles. The Jackson family dominated the R&B charts in the late 1960s and '70s, before Michael and Janet Jackson took the world by storm with their solo work. More recently, hard rock and heavy metal have produced two huge Indiana artists—David Lee Roth, with the legendary band Van Halen, and Axl Rose of the equally legendary Guns N' Roses. It's a long way from the witty, high-society lyrics of Cole Porter to the primal screams and wailing guitars of Roth and Rose, but that is what makes the Indiana music scene so vital. It evolves with the times and allows superstars to emerge and dazzle the entire world.

Hoagy Carmichael, born in Bloomington, Indiana, was an accomplished composer, singer, bandleader, pianist, and actor.

War II war correspondents. His first wartime assignment was covering the London Blitz bombings of 1940. Subsequently, he reported on battles in Sicily, Italy, and France, often writing about the experiences of ordinary soldiers. Pyle was killed by Japanese fire during the Okinawa campaign.

Kurt Vonnegut Jr. (1922– 2007) Author Kurt Vonnegut Jr. grew up in Indianapolis and enlisted in the U.S. Army during World War II. He was captured by the Germans in 1944 and was held for a year as a prisoner of war (POW). Vonnegut's novels are dark and satirical, and they often include elements of science fiction. His 1969 masterpiece, *Slaughterhouse-Five,* was based on his experience as a POW during the Allied firebombing of Dresden.

Kurt Vonnegut, celebrated author of *Slaughterhouse-Five* and *Cat's Cradle,* was born in Indianapolis.

Twyla Tharp (1941–) Born in Portland, Indiana, dancer and choreographer Twyla Tharp has choreographed dance works for many great dance companies. She founded her own company, Twyla Tharp Dance, in 1965. Tharp has also worked in television, film (*Hair* and *Amadeus*), and theater, winning two Emmy Awards and a Tony Award.

Actors, Athletes, and Entertainers

Steve McQueen (1930–1980) Actor Steve McQueen, born in Indiana, earned the nickname the King of Cool for his portrayal of silent loners in a number of blockbuster movies in the 1960s and 1970s. He is best known for the *Great Escape*, *The Thomas Crown Affair*, and *Bullitt*.

James Dean appears in a photo for the 1955 movie *Rebel Without a Cause*. He died that same year.

James Dean (1931–1955) Indiana native James Dean was a talented young actor who portrayed frustrated, idealistic youth in his major movie roles. He starred in *East of Eden*, *Rebel Without a Cause*, and *Giant*. After his early death in a car accident, Dean became a movie icon.

Larry Bird (1956–) Basketball superstar Larry Bird played for Indiana State University and joined the Boston Celtics in 1980. He helped lead his team to National Basketball Association (NBA) championships in 1981, 1984, and 1986. He was named the NBA's

Larry Bird was born and raised in Indiana. After a famed career playing for Indiana State University and the Boston Celtics, he became coach and then president of the Indiana Pacers.

Most Valuable Player in 1984, 1985, and 1986. Bird also cocaptained the American basketball team in the 1992 Olympics and was coach of the Indiana Pacers from 1997 to 2000.

John Mellencamp (1951–) Hoosier John Mellencamp is a popular and critically acclaimed musician best known for catchy heartland rock songs with a social message. Mellencamp's hits include songs like "Hurts So Good" and "Pink Houses." Mellencamp is also one of the founders of Farm Aid, the concert series that raises money for farm families.

The Jackson Family The Jackson 5, from Gary, was a musical group made up of brothers Jackie, Tito, Jermaine (later replaced by younger brother Randy), Marlon, and Michael. They were an R&B/pop sensation of the 1970s. Michael (1958–2009) went on to become a superstar of the 1980s with albums such as *Off the Wall*, *Thriller*, and *Bad*. A Jackson sister, Janet (1966–), also established a highly successful solo career as a pop singer. On June 25, 2009, Michael Jackson died suddenly at his home in Los Angeles, California, at the age of fifty. He was just weeks away from a scheduled series of farewell concerts to be held in London, England. A large and emotional memorial service was held for Jackson at the Staples Center in Los Angeles. In addition to ordinary fans, the service was attended by music and entertainment industry luminaries like Stevie Wonder, Lionel Richie, Mariah Carey, Jennifer Hudson, Usher, Berry Gordy (founder of Motown Records), Smokey Robinson, Queen Latifah, and the poet Maya Angelou.

Timeline

15000 BCE–1600 CE A succession of different Native American peoples occupy present-day Indiana.

1679 La Salle explores Indiana.

1717 The French establish the first trading post in Indiana.

1763 The French cede their North American territory to the British. Pontiac's Rebellion fails.

1778 George Rogers Clark captures Vincennes from the British.

1787 The Northwest Territory is established.

1794 An American force defeats a confederacy of Native American tribes at the Battle of Fallen Timbers.

1800 The Indiana Territory is created.

1811 William Henry Harrison defeats Native American forces at the battle of Tippecanoe.

1812 Tecumseh is killed in a battle during the War of 1812.

1816 Indiana becomes the nineteenth state.

1825 Indianapolis becomes the state capital.

1841 William Henry Harrison is elected president.

1863 John Hunt Morgan invades Indiana during the Civil War.

1888 Benjamin Harrison is elected president.

1909 U.S. Steel Corporation opens a plant in Gary.

1911 The first Indianapolis 500 is held.

1966 Indiana Dunes National Lakeshore is established.

1967 Richard G. Hatcher is elected mayor of Gary, making him Indiana's first African American mayor.

2009 Indiana native and King of Pop Michael Jackson dies at the age of fifty.

State motto	"The Crossroads of America"
State capital	Indianapolis
State bird	Cardinal
State tree	Tulip tree, also called tulip poplar
State flower	Peony
State stone	Salem limestone
Statehood date and number	1816; nineteenth state
State nickname	Hoosier State
Total area and U.S. rank	36,291 square miles (93,993 sq km); thirty-eighth
Population	6,345,289
Length of coastline	Lake Michigan coastline—45 miles (72 km)
Highest elevation	Hoosier Hill, at 1,257 feet (383 m)
Lowest elevation	Ohio River, at 325 feet (98 m)

State Flag

State Seal

Major rivers	Wabash, Big Blue, Calumet, Eel, Elkhart, Iroquois, Kankakee, Maumee, Ohio, Patoka, Saint Joseph, Tippecanoe, White, Whitewater
Major lakes	Michigan, Brookeville, Freeman, Manitou, Monroe, Patoka, Prairie Creek, Raccoon, Salamonie, Shafer, Tippecanoe, Wawasee, Maxinkuckee
Hottest temperature recorded	116 degrees Fahrenheit (47 degrees Celsius), at Collegeville, July 14, 1936
Coldest temperature recorded	-36°F (-38°C), at New Whiteland, January 19, 1994
Origin of state name	Indiana means "Land of Indians"
Chief agricultural products	Corn, soybeans, pork, chicken and eggs, cattle and dairy products, wheat, hay, vegetables, apples and other fruit
Major industries	Steel and metal goods, transportation equipment, chemicals

Cardinal

Peony

agronomy The application of soil and plant sciences to soil management and crop production.

canal An artificial waterway or artificially improved river used for irrigation, shipping, or transportation.

confederacy People, groups, or nations united for some common purpose; a league or alliance formed by such a union.

constitution The system of fundamental laws and principles that lays out and describes the nature, functions, and limits of a government or other institution.

counterattack A military offensive by troops who previously have been defending a position; a switch from a defensive position (defending against an attack) to an offensive one (going on the attack).

cultivate To raise or produce a crop.

dune A hill or ridge of windblown sand.

ecosystem A system formed by a community of organisms and their interactions with their physical environment.

electoral vote The vote cast in a presidential election by the electoral college, the body of electors made up of representatives from each state.

frontier A region at the edge of a country's inhabited, established, and developed population centers, outside of and beyond a country's cities, towns, and villages.

glacier A mass of ice that slowly moves over a landmass.

limestone A sedimentary rock consisting mainly of calcium carbonate, formed by the remains of marine organisms.

pottery Earthenware vessels such as vases or bowls that are shaped from clay and then baked in a kiln or oven.

quarry An open excavation or pit where stone is extracted.

steel mill A plant where steel is manufactured from raw materials.

territory A part of the United States that is not a state but is administered by a separate governor and legislature.

treaty A formal agreement between two or more states.

FOR MORE INFORMATION

Children's Museum of Indianapolis

3000 North Meridian Street

Indianapolis, IN 46208

(317) 334-3322

Web site: http://www.childrensmuseum.org

This museum houses eleven major galleries that explore the physical and natural sciences, history, world cultures, and the arts, emphasizing exhibits that are "hands-on" or participatory in nature.

Historic Landmarks Foundation of Indiana

340 West Michigan Street

Indianapolis, IN 46202

(317) 639-4534

Web site: http://www.historiclandmarks.org

The Historic Landmarks Foundation of Indiana saves and restores the state's historic places.

Indiana Dunes National Lakeshore (U.S. National Parks Service)

1100 North Mineral Springs Road

Porter, IN 46304

(219) 926-7561

Web site: http://www.nps.gov/indu/index.htm

This national park's Web site features news and information on the Indiana Dunes National Lakeshore.

Indiana Historical Society

Eugene and Marilyn Glick Indiana History Center

450 West Ohio Street

Indianapolis, IN 46202

(317) 232-1882

Web site: http://www.indianahistory.org

This organization, founded in 1830, is dedicated to collecting, preserving, interpreting, and disseminating Indiana history.

Indianapolis 500

4790 West 16th Street

Indianapolis, IN 46222

Web site: http://www.indy500.com

The race organization's Web site offers news and information on the "Greatest Spectacle in Racing."

Visit Indiana

Indiana Office of Tourism Development

One North Capitol, Suite 600

Indianapolis, IN 46204-2288

(800) 677-9800

Web site: http://www.in.gov/visitindiana

This is Indiana's official department of tourism.

Web sites

Due to the changing nature of Internet links, Rosen Publishing has developed an online list of Web sites related to the subject of this book. This site is updated regularly. Please use this link to access this list:

http://www.rosenlinks.com/uspp/inpp

Brill, Marlene Targ. *Indiana*. New York, NY: Marshall Cavendish Benchmark, 2006.

Collier, Kristi. *Throwing Stones*. New York, NY: Henry Holt, 2006.

Conn, Earl L. *My Indiana: 101 Places to See*. Indianapolis, IN: Indiana Historical Society Press, 2006.

Heinrichs, Ann. *Indiana*. Minneapolis, MN: Compass Point Books, 2004.

Marimen, Mark, et al. *Weird Indiana: Your Travel Guide to Indiana's Local Legends and Best Kept Secrets*. New York, NY: Sterling, 2008.

Mazer, Harry. *My Brother Abe: Sally Lincoln's Story*. New York, NY: Simon & Schuster Books for Young Readers, 2009.

Molzahn, Arlene Bourgeois. *La Salle: Explorer of the Mississippi*. Berkeley Heights, NJ: Enslow Elementary, 2004.

Moore, Anne Chieko. *Benjamin Harrison: Centennial President*. Commack, NY: Nova Science Publishers, 2009.

Peck, Richard. *Here Lies the Librarian*. New York, NY: Dial Books, 2006.

Perry, George C. *James Dean*. New York, NY: DK Publishing, 2005.

Pimm, Nancy Roe. *Indy 500: The Inside Track*. Plain City, OH: Darby Creek Publishing, 2004.

Queen, Mary Jane Child. *William Henry Harrison: General and President*. Commack, NY: Nova Science Publishers, 2006.

Sanders, Scott Russell, and Rich Clark. *Wild and Scenic Indiana*. San Francisco, CA: Browntrout Publishers, 2005.

Stille, Darlene R. *Indiana*. New York, NY: Children's Press, 2008.

Stratton-Porter, Gene. *Freckles*. Winnetka, CA: Norilana Books, 2006.

Teale, Edwin Way. *Dune Boy: The Early Years of a Naturalist*. Storrs, CT: Bibliopola Press, 2002.

Thrasher, Crystal. *The Dark Didn't Catch Me*. Bloomington, IN: Indiana University Press, 2004.

Wilkie, Katharine E. *George Rogers Clark: Boy of the Northwest Frontier*. Carmel, IN: Patria Press, Inc., 2004.

BIBLIOGRAPHY

Dufrene, Uric, and James Altmann. "The Professional and Business Services Sector: Employment Changes Across Indiana Metros." *Indiana Business Review*, 2007. Retrieved April 2009 (http://www.ibrc.indiana.edu/IBR/2007/summer/article1.html).

Esarey, Logan. *The Indiana Home*. Bloomington, IN: Indiana University Press, 1976.

Furlong, Patrick J. *Indiana: An Illustrated History*. Northridge, CA: Windsor Publications, Inc., 1985.

Hoover, Dwight W., with Jane Rodman. *A Pictorial History of Indiana*. Bloomington, IN: Indiana University Press, 1980.

Indianapolis Star. "History of the Indy 500." Retrieved April 2009. (http://www.indystar.com/apps/pbcs.dll/article?AID=/99999999/NEWS06/80508054&template=theme&theme=starfiles_indy500history).

Johnson, Howard. *A Home in the Woods: Pioneer Life in Indiana*. Bloomington, IN: Indiana University Press, 1991.

Madison, James H. *The Indiana Way: A State History*. Bloomington, IN: Indiana University Press, 1990.

Peckham, Howard H. *Indiana: A History*. Urbana, IL: University of Illinois Press, 2003.

Pollan, Michael. *The Botany of Desire: A Plant's-Eye View of the World*. Waterville, ME: G. K. Hall & Co., 2001.

Skertic, Mark. *A Native's Guide to Northwest Indiana*. Chicago, IL: Lake Claremont Press, 2003.

Thomas, Phyllis. *Indiana Off the Beaten Path: A Guide to Unique Places*. 8th ed. Guilford, CT: Insiders' Guide, 2005.

INDEX

About the Author

Corona Brezina has written more than a dozen titles for Rosen Publishing. Several of her previous books have focused on topics related to American history and current events, including *Sojourner Truth's "Aint I a Woman"* and *Climate Change*. She lives in Chicago, Illinois, and has long enjoyed occasional weekend getaways to the beautiful Indiana Dunes.

Photo Credits

Cover (top left) Margaret Bourke-White/Time & Life Pictures/Getty Images; cover (top right), p. 21 Shutterstock.com; cover (bottom) Robert Laberge/Getty Images; pp. 3, 6, 13, 22, 26, 32, 39 © www.istockphoto.com/Mark Evans; p. 4 (top) © GeoAtlas; pp. 7, 30 © David R. Frazier Photolibrary, Inc./Alamy; p. 10 Bruce Forster/Stone/Getty Images; p. 12 © www.istockphoto.com/Steve Geer; p. 14 Archive Photos/Getty Images; p. 16 © North Wind Picture Archives/Alamy; p. 20 Indiana State Archives; pp. 23, 25, 41 (right) Wikimedia Commons; pp. 24 (left), 36 Hulton Archive/Getty Images; p. 24 (right) Getty Images, Courtesy of the National Archives; p. 27 © Cameron Davidson/Alamy; p. 29 Gene Peach/Riser/ Getty Images; p. 33 AFP/Getty Images; p. 34 George Konig/Hulton Archive/Getty Images; p. 35 Mark Mainz/Getty Images; p. 37 Matt Campbell/AFP/Getty Images; p. 40 (left) Courtesy of Robesus Inc.; p. 41 (left) Wikimedia Commons from the U.S. Fish and Wildlife Service.

Designer: Les Kanturek; Photo Researcher: Cindy Reiman